Topics in Context

Context

Being Young – Joys and Challenges

Themenheft

Cornelsen

Context

Being Young – Joys and Challenges

Im Auftrag des Verlages herausgegeben von
Dr. Annette Leithner-Brauns, Dresden

Erarbeitet von
Martina Baasner, Berlin; Irene Bartscherer, Bonn; Lisa Braun, Meppen; Dr. Sabine Buchholz, Hürth; Wiebke Bettina Dietrich, Göttingen; Sylvia Loh, Esslingen; Benjamin Lorenz, Bensheim; Dr. Paul Maloney, Hildesheim; Dr. Pascal Ohlmann, Tholey; Birgit Ohmsieder, Berlin; Dr. Andreas Sedlatschek, Esslingen; Veronika Walther, Rudolstadt

In Zusammenarbeit mit der Englischredaktion
Dr. Marion Kiffe (Koordinierende Redakteurin), Dr. Christiane Kallenbach (Projektleitung), Aryane Beaudoin, Dr. Jan Dreßler, Hartmut Tschepe, Dr. Christian von Raumer, Freya Wurm *unter Mitwirkung von* Janan Barksdale, Irja Fröhling, Katrin Gütermann, Anne Müller, Neil Porter, Evelyn Sternad, Mai Weber

Beratende Mitwirkung
Ramin Azadian, Berlin; Heiko Benzin, Neustrelitz; Sabine Otto, Halle (Saale)

Layoutkonzept
Klein & Halm, Berlin

Layout und technische Umsetzung
Straive
designcollective, Berlin

Umschlaggestaltung
Rosendahl, Berlin

Lizenzmanagement
Britta Bensmann

Weitere Bestandteile des Lehrwerks

- *Schulbuch* (print und als E-Book)
- *E-Books* (in zwei Varianten: 1. alle *Topics in Context* bzw. 2. Schulbuch und *Topics in Context*)
- *Lehrkräftefassung des Schulbuchs* (im Unterrichtsmanager)
- *Handreichungen für den Unterricht* (print und im Unterrichtsmanager)
- *Workbook* (print)
- *Unterrichtsmanager*
- *Vorschläge zur Leistungsmessung* (digital)
- *Cornelsen Lernen App*

www.cornelsen.de

1. Auflage, 1. Druck 2022

Alle Drucke dieser Auflage sind inhaltlich unverändert und können im Unterricht nebeneinander verwendet werden.

Druck: H. Heenemann, Berlin

ISBN 978-3-06-036525-8

PEFC
PEFC/04-31-1156

PEFC zertifiziert
Dieses Produkt stammt aus nachhaltig bewirtschafteten Wäldern und kontrollierten Quellen.

www.pefc.de

Being Young – Joys and Challenges

A

D

1 **a** Look at the pictures. Decide which pictures best represent your ideas of being young.

b Discuss your choices with a partner and agree on three pictures that both of you consider characteristic of youth. Add convincing *headings for them.

2 **a** Copy and fill in the table below. Refer to the pictures first, then add ideas of your own.

Present joys	Present worries	Future hopes	Future fears
...	...	...	...

b Add to your table as you work on the texts in this chapter.

3 ***Quick write:** Look at the Chapter map on the right. Refer to the topics listed there and do a quick write on your initial spontaneous reaction to the guiding question.

Chapter map

Youth issues: Who am I, and who will I be?

- Generation Z
- relationships
- youth culture(s)
- eternal youth
- beauty ideals
- life after school
- social media

Chapter task: a message

▸ More language

Adolescence: an in-between phase

Youth – or adolescence – is the stage of life between childhood and adulthood. During this phase, adolescents undergo physiological and psychological changes that eventually prepare them for their adult lives, with all the legal and social issues this implies.

Youth and society

It may seem that 'youth' is a universal category that has always existed in all cultures around the world. But this is not the case: In many cultures, adolescents used to be or still are treated like grown-ups, leaving no room for the lifestyles and experiences usually attributed to young people.

In most modern Western societies, however, 'youth' does exist as an independent phase in a person's life. Here, adolescence is a phase in which young people are allowed to experiment with and explore different possibilities before eventually making a commitment e.g. to values, a profession, or a partner. Birthday parties, school proms or a driver's licence can be considered modern rites of passage that mark young people's coming of age and celebrate their independence.

While their peer group becomes more important for young people, their relationship with their parents may be affected by conflict and distancing. Such conflicts between members of different generations, the so-called 'generation gap', often result from contrasting perspectives on life. Types of behaviour that are considered rebellious or nonconformist by the older generation may evolve into distinctive forms of youth culture that show their creative potential by setting trends or influencing public discourse.

Challenges

Despite the liberties of youth, coming of age is often experienced as a period of inner turmoil – or 'teenage angst'. Factors such as uncertainty about their appearance, peer pressure and fear of social exclusion may lead young people to greater risk-taking e.g. by experimenting with drugs or in their sexual activities. Their need to seek praise, especially in social media, can turn into an obsession with self-optimization. This may lead to self-doubt and low self-esteem rather than to body positivity. Ongoing frustration with unattainable ideals may eventually result in serious health conditions such as depression or eating disorders.

Future plans

Finishing school is undoubtedly a major milestone on the path to adulthood. Depending on their qualifications and interests, school leavers can enrol at university or a further education college, become an apprentice or start vocational training. Others take up an internship before they commit to a career path, or they take a gap year in order to travel, engage in voluntary work or simply to find out where their interests lie. Whatever decisions young people make, these may or may not turn out to be the right ones for their future. But it is always possible to make new decisions and head in a different direction.

1 Words words words

Work in groups of three, with each person concentrating on one of the three major paragraphs in the text.

a Prepare a short oral summary of your paragraph. From the highlighted words in the text choose three that you find central to your paragraph and use them in your summary.

b Present your summaries to each other. While listening, note down useful words.

c Compare your lists of words and add words from your partners' lists to yours.

d Choose three words and explain them to your partners, e.g. by paraphrasing or defining them or by using synonyms or antonyms. Let your partners guess the words.

2 Mind mapping

a Draw a mind map containing the words from **1**.

b Go through the text again and add further words to your mind map.

3 Chunk it!

a In the text, the following words go together with other words to form *chunks. Identify them:

1 ... changes (l. 2)
2 ... perspectives (l. 18)
3 ... praise (l. 26)
4 ... ideals (l. 29)
5 ... internship (l. 35)

b For each gap in **a** think of at least two more words to form chunks.

c Look for possible chunks for ten other words from **2**, either in the text or in a dictionary. Add them to your mind map.

► Getting started

► Check

4 Defining youth

You choose Work on either task **a** or **b**. Use as many words from tasks **1–3** as you can.

a Discuss with a partner to what extent the ideas in the text match your own concept of youth.
► Language help

b Writing Write a short definition of the term *adulthood*. It can be serious or funny.

Language help

contrast with sth. • correspond to sth. • contradict sth. • match sth. • doubt sth. • (dis)agree with sth. • object to the idea that ... • hold/have a different view / the same view as sb. • be of the same opinion as sb.

Youth cultures throughout history

- Look at the pictures below and say which of them represent the concept of freedom, youthful rebellion and/or nonconformity best.
- Compare your choice with a partner. Confirm or revise your original choice and explain your reasons.

Info

Between childhood and adulthood: youth culture

It may sound surprising that 'youth' as a distinct phase between childhood and adulthood is not universal across all human societies. Where there is no youth culture, children are expected to behave as adults as soon as they are physically and intellectually able to do so.

Independent youth cultures tend to be a phenomenon of modern industrialized societies, and they are generally believed to have emerged in the 20th century. Sociologists regard compulsory schooling as a major reason for the formation of a youth culture: At school, adolescents mainly interact with other young people, which means an independent culture can develop. Adolescents who do not attend school mostly live among grown-ups and tend to adopt adult norms and values.

Youth cultures strive to set themselves apart from the parental generation. Areas in which adolescents differ from their parents can be values and norms, musical tastes, clothing styles, interests and even the way they use language: They may use words differently from grown-ups, or use different words altogether.

Youth cultures also tend to diversify, which means that there is not only one, but many youth cultures at any one time. While this diversification may help adolescents find a peer group that suits their personality, it also often leads to animosity between youth cultures. For example, in Britain in the 1970s, there were frequent violent clashes between mods and rockers. The 1980s brought about a diversification of youth tribes. Often, depending on their musical preferences, New Romantics, Metal-heads, Yuppies, New-wavers, Rastas existed side by side.

1 Referring to youth cultures of the past or the present, give examples of how they may differ from that of the older generation in terms of values, clothing and musical tastes.

Comprehension

1 Listening Listen to three soundbites about youth cultures in the 1970s and 1980s. Make notes on

1 what mods would wear
2 what role Jean-Paul Belmondo played for mods
3 what could happen if you went to a punk concert
4 how rockers felt when they met mods.

Annotations
run the gauntlet *Spießruten laufen*

► Check

► SF 38: Listening/Viewing for gist and detail, Student's book p. 314

Beyond the text

2 You choose Work on either task **a** or **b**.

a Writing Write a short *blog post on the advantages and downsides of belonging to a youth culture.

b Speaking Do youth cultures still exist today? Give a 2-minute talk.

► SF 27: Writing a blog post, Student's book p. 300

Generation Z – are the kids alright? Nosheen Iqbal

Info

The Baby Boomers (born 1965–1969)

Generation X (born 1969–1981)

Millennials / Generation Y (born 1982–1995)

Generation Z (born 1996–2015)

Generation Alpha (succeeded Gen Z)

- **Think** What do you associate with being young? Collect at least five ideas. You might think of interests, activities, peer group and social relations, attitudes and style, privileges, challenges etc.
- **Pair** Compare ideas with a partner and agree on five concepts that both of you consider characteristic of your generation.
- **Share** Share ideas with another pair of students and write a portrait of your generation. Reflect on how your views on the guiding question may have changed.

Now read what some British teenagers consider typical of Generation Z.

They drink less, take far fewer drugs, and have made teenage pregnancy a near anomaly. Generation Z – one of several terms used to describe post-millennial youth born after 1996 – prefer juice bars to pub crawls, rank quality family time ahead of sex and prioritise good grades before friendship, at least according to a report published by the British Pregnancy Advisory Service [...].

An onslaught of sneering headlines followed, characterising today's youth as boring, sensible and hopelessly screen-addicted.

So, are the kids all right?

'We have so much more to do than [just] drink and take drugs,' says Demi Babalola, a 19-year-old philosophy and sociology student. 'I'm not surprised those [statistics] show that's the case: it makes sense. We have a lot more to distract us now.'

What's her biggest time stealer? 'Social media.' Babalola toggles between Snapchat, Twitter and Instagram, although she rolls her eyes at the mention of Facebook, full as it is of 'older people'.

But it's not just the breadth of entertainment and culture that is so instantly available – and disposable – to Babalola and her peers. There is also a growing feeling that the preoccupations of her parents' generation seem, well, a bit lame.

'Going out takes a lot of effort: it's boring, repetitive and expensive,' she says. 'Obviously, I used to go out a lot in my first year [at university], but now we do more kickbacks.'

To the uninitiated, a kickback is the sophisticated Gen Z sweet spot between the lairy house parties of yore – the ones typified by vomit on the parental carpet and a trashing of the family bathroom – and a pre-teen sleepover.

'We hang out, we listen to music, make our own food, and play games,' she says. 'We'll probably organise it a couple of days before.'

Lewis Allely, 14, from Cornwall, agrees. 'We're quite different [from your generation] because there's more stuff to do at each other's houses and we have more technology – like, we have video games.' [...]

The cliche that many young people spend far too much time online, instead of indulging in a romanticised form of rebellion, may have some truth, but as futurologist Rhiannon McGregor points out, Gen Z-ers are more cautious and risk-averse than their parents, partly because that technology exists.

'They're aware from an early age of how they're portrayed online and offline, so they curate themselves in a more conservative way,' she says. (In other words, no one wants to be publicly shamed getting messy or being recklessly daft.)

Annotations
- 2 **anomaly** sth. that is unusual/uncommon
- 3 **pub crawl** act of visiting several pubs and consuming drinks
- 7 **onslaught** (here) a rush of messages
- 7 **sneering** sarcastic
- 14 **toggle between x and y** (here) switch from one application to another
- 18 **disposable** not really needed
- 19 **preoccupation** worry
- 23 **the uninitiated** *(humorous)* inexperienced people
- 23 **sweet spot** (here) optimum combination
- 24 **lairy** (here) loud and exciting
- 24 **of yore** *(humorous)* in the past
- 32 **indulge in sth.** enjoy sth.
- 33 **risk-averse** not willing to take risks
- 36 **curate yourself** (here) present yourself online
- 37 **daft** *(infml)* silly

'But they're also more socially aware and see themselves as part of a global community. It's easier to get and feel connected to someone in Africa or Asia and share concerns about climate change, for instance.'

Clara Finnigan, 22, who grew up in Devon and is in her final year at the University of Arts London, points out that one size doesn't fit all. She still goes out, 'often to gay clubs'.

She believes her generation is unfairly judged and that it reports levels of stress and depression that are higher than ever because of the economic and political state of the world it has inherited.

'The whole anxiety of not having stability in your future is something that is definitely very present. I won't probably ever own my own house, unless I get really lucky.' [...] 'I don't expect to have one full-time gig; my career won't be defined by one job. I know I'll have to do stuff I don't enjoy to be able to do passion projects that I do.' [...]

The subjects of Brexit and of dropping out of university to pursue less mind-bogglingly expensive apprenticeships come up a lot. As does a consistent refusal to accept that anyone should be defined by traditional markers of identity.

'We're more inclusive,' says Babalola. 'You can do what you want as long as you don't harm anyone and stay safe. It's about freedom. Previous generations always made distinct separations between being gay or straight.

'I try to avoid labels – being a black girl means society already has certain stereotypes that are expected, like I should be outspoken or "sassy" or loud or like certain music.' Another eyeroll. 'It's restricting.' [...]

While statistics show that smoking, drinking and clubbing may be in decline for today's young people, the health and wellness industry is booming with the same demographic – in part because these young people have had so much information at their disposal. [...] Generation Z-ers will, after all, be living longer and more healthily, and looking better for it.

A report from the Institute of Alcohol Studies suggests that changing demographics also play a part, reporting that 'ethnic minority children ... are less likely to drink, [which] can directly explain a small proportion of the fall in underage drinking' but also that there is evidence these same minority students can also influence their peers. 'Non-Muslim children in schools with a high Muslim population are less likely to drink,' it states.

So what is the new going out? The Generation Z idea of fun that is inexplicable to older adults? [...] Allely and Babalola instantly refer me to Snapchat, where they communicate in a constant group feed with their friends. Broadcasting the minutiae of her day – a good oufit, a trip to Westfield – is as second nature as breathing to Babalola.

'It's kind of documenting your life, but you have an audience and you immediately know who's interacting. I enjoy it – it makes me feel important that 100 people are watching what I'm eating.' [...] And what are Babalola's plans for today? 'My friends and I go out to London, or cycling. We might go to a cute cafe and take pictures.'

From: 'Generation Z: "We have more to do than drink and take drugs"', theguardian.com *21 July 2018*

Annotations

- 50 **anxiety** fearfulness, nervousness
- 52 **gig** *(AE)* job
- 55 **pursue sth.** (here) engage in sth.
- 56 **mind-boggling** very surprising
- 56 **apprenticeship** *Ausbildung*
- 61 **label** *(n)* (here) attachment of characteristics to a person or group in order to define them
- 62 **sassy** *(AE infml)* bold and lively
- 64 **be in decline** become less frequent
- 66 **demographic** *(n)* section of a society that shares certain features
- 77 **minutiae** [maɪˈnjuːʃiaɪ] *(pl)* precise details
- 78 **Westfield** shopping centre in London

Comprehension

1 Point out how Generation Z is described in the report mentioned, by the media and by some of its representatives.

2 Sum up the differences between Generation Z and older generations as presented in the text.

Analysis

► SF 17: Reading and understanding non-fictional texts, Student's book p. 285

3 Examine Nosheen Iqbal's attitude towards Generation Z. Consider the language, style and structure of her article.

Language awareness

► Getting started

4 This portrayal of Generation Z makes frequent use of colloquial language, especially when somebody is quoted. List five examples and rewrite them in a more formal register.

Beyond the text

► Getting started
► SF 26: Argumentative writing: discussion and comment, Student's book p. 298
► SF 35: Writing a letter to the editor, Student's book, p. 310

5 You choose Writing Work on either task **a** or **b**.

a Is today's youth 'boring, sensible and hopelessly screen-addicted' (l. 7)? Write a letter to the editor expressing your view on this quote.

b Leave a comment on the newspaper's website calling for greater tolerance and understanding of Generation Z-ers.

Language help

(fully) agree with ... • be of the same opinion as • I think it's true that ... • be convinced that ... • wonder if you should rather... • Couldn't it be that... • doubt if ... • not agree at all • see the point in ... • I feel I need to contradict

Is 'OK, Boomer' ok, Boomer? Rezo

- Can you think of a typical phrase, greeting or joke used by your generation? What does it mean? Do you use it too?

On the website of the German weekly Die Zeit, *German social media influencer Rezo defends young people using 'OK, boomer' to silence older people who treat them without respect.*

Liebe ZEIT-ONLINE-Leser, heute habe ich gleich zu Beginn mal eine Frage: Wurdet Ihr zwischen 1955 und 1969 geboren, gehört also zu einem der Jahrgänge der deutschen Babyboomergeneration? Dann habe ich für Euch jetzt eine harte Wahrheit: Es ist völlig okay, wenn Leute irrationale und respektlose Statements von Euch mit „OK, Boomer" abqualifizieren. Nicht nur das: Es ist sogar ziemlich heilsam und wichtig, dass Euch das passiert. Denn „OK, Boomer" ist mehr als nachvollziehbar und noch extrem lieb und konstruktiv gegenüber dem, was die mächtige und privilegierte Boomergeneration, Eure Generation, den Jüngeren ständig vor den Kopf knallt.

Warum, das möchte ich Euch jetzt – wie gewohnt logisch (lol) – beweisen. Dafür werde ich Euch natürlich erst einmal erklären, was es mit „OK, Boomer" auf sich hat. „OK, Boomer" (oder „Ok, Boomer" oder „OK Boomer") ist ein Meme, das seit ein paar Monaten im Internet immer häufiger benutzt wird. Ein Meme ist im Regelfall ein humoristisches oder satirisches Bild oder kurzes Video, welches auf eine den Zuschauern bekannte und in dem Kulturraum wiederkehrende Pointe zurückgreift. In diesem Fall ist die Pointe, dass auf unnötig belehrendes, abschätziges oder weltfremdes Verhalten von Boomern schlicht mit einem nüchternen „OK, Boomer" reagiert wird.

Die jüngste Popularität von „OK, Boomer" (oder „Ok, Boomer" oder „OK Boomer") kann in erster Linie auf zwei virale Quellen zurückgeführt werden. Zum einen ist da das Video einer neuseeländischen Parlamentarierin, die während ihrer Rede Zwischenrufe älterer weißer männlicher Kollegen mit einem nüchternen „Okay, Boomer" zum Schweigen brachte. Zum anderen sind da auch virale TikTok-Videos (das ist eine neue Social-Media-Plattform aus China), in denen auf despektierliche Moves von Boomern reagiert wird. Wie zum Beispiel auf einen Boomer, welcher jüngere Generationen in einem ausführlichen Rant angreift und durch falsche Unterstellungen und Verallgemeinerungen schlecht darstellen möchte. In beiden Fällen stellt „OK, Boomer" (und so fort) also eine simple Antwort auf respektloses und geringschätziges Verhalten dar, ohne sich auf das Niveau des Angreifers herabzulassen. Natürlich gibt es bestimmt auch einzelne Fälle, bei denen der Ausdruck unpassend und unnötig abfällig genutzt wird. Die viralen Trends, der zugrunde liegende Joke und unzählige reichweitenstarke Beispiele tun dies allerdings nicht.

Dass dennoch manche (!) Boomer allein durch diese Bezeichnung ein flaues Gefühl im Magen bekommen, hat viel eher etwas mit dem Verlust des Status quo im öffentlichen Diskurs zu tun. Für alle anderen Generationen ist es völlig normal, dass über sie als Gruppe gesprochen wird. Zeitungen denken und sprechen meist aus der Perspektive der Alten, die für die Jungen irgendwelche Labels wie „Millennials" oder „Gen Z" erfinden. Wenn Boomer die Zeitung dann zuschlagen und den Fernseher anmachen, erfahren sie die Einordnung der aktuellen Themen von Influencerinnen wie Sandra Maischberger (Boomerin), Frank Plasberg

Info

Rezo (born 1992) is a German vlogger and social media influencer. He publishes on his video channels and is well known for his outspoken political criticism.

▶ More info

(Boomer), Anne Will (Boomerin), Maybrit Illner (Boomerin) oder Markus Lanz (Boomer). Der ZDF-Fernsehrat – nur als Beispiel für den öffentlich-rechtlichen Rundfunk – besteht zu 58 Prozent aus Boomern und neben dieser Gruppe gibt es mehr Mitglieder im gesetzlichen Rentenalter als Mitglieder unter 50 Jahren. Fun Fact am Rande: Der ZDF-Fernsehrat beschreibt seine Mitglieder als „so vielfältig wie die Gesellschaft selbst“ ... lol, OK, Boomer (guckt, so funktioniert das Meme). [...]

Am Ende, liebe Boomer, kann ich verstehen, wenn sich „OK, Boomer“ merkwürdig anfühlt. Und es ist nicht cool, wenn Leute diesen Spruch an den falschen Stellen benutzen, um den Gesprächspartner mundtot zu machen. Aber eigentlich sind diese zwei Worte lediglich Ausdruck kollektiver Erschöpfung von Generationen, die durch konstruktives demokratisches Verhalten ständig auf irrationale Politik der Boomer stoßen, deren zerstörerische Folgen nicht die Alten, sondern die Jungen ertragen müssen. [...]

Also seht es uns nach, wenn wir einmal zu oft genervt „OK, Boomer“ sagen. Es ist ja auch nervig, kein Boomer zu sein. Peace.

From: '"OK, Boomer" ist okay, Boomer!', Die Zeit, *20 November 2019*

► Getting started

► Support p. 26
► SF 47: Mediating from German into English, Student's book p. 332

1 Mediating You and your English friend hear a young man saying 'OK Boomer' to an older man. Your friend finds this very impolite. Tell him why – according to Rezo – this phrase might have been justified.

Text 4

► More info

Someone desirable

Nick Hornby

- What makes somebody desirable? With another student, take turns asking each other the 'This or that' questions below. For any question, you have to pick one of the given options and explain your choice.

  - Call or text?
  - Snapchat or TikTok?
  - Sport or books?
  - Jeans or sweats?
  - Chatting or silence?
  - Introvert or extrovert?
  - Long hair or short hair?
  - Alternative or mainstream?
  - Going out or staying in?
  - Nice friends or nice parents?
  - Mutual hobbies or mutual friends?
  - Good looks or clever conversation?
  - A good sport or an idol on a pedestal?
  - Same taste in music or same taste in food?

In this excerpt from Nick Hornby's novel High Fidelity, *Rob Fleming, the novel's narrator, recalls when he fell in love with Charlie Nicholson.*

I met Charlie at tech: I was doing a media studies course, and she was studying design, and when I first saw her I realized she was the sort of girl I had wanted to meet ever since I'd been old enough to want to meet girls. She was tall, with blonde cropped hair (she said she knew some people who were at St Martin's with some friends of Johnny Rotten, but I was never introduced to them), and she looked different and dramatic and exotic. Even her name seemed to me dramatic and dif-

Annotations
1 **tech** technical college
4 **cropped** very short
4 **St Martin's** college of the University of the Arts in London
5 **Johnny Rotten** (born 1956) stage name of John Joseph Lydon, the singer of the Sex Pistols, a British punk band active between 1975 and 1978

ferent and exotic, because up until then I had lived in a world where girls had girls' names, and not very interesting ones at that. She talked a lot, so that you didn't have those terrible, strained silences that seemed to characterize most of my sixth-form dates, and when she talked she said remarkably interesting things – about her course, about my course, about music, about films and books and politics.
And she liked me. She liked *me*. *She* liked me. She *liked* me. Or at least, I think she did. I *think* she did. Etc. I have never been entirely sure what it is women like about me, but I know that ardour helps (even I know how difficult it is to resist someone who finds you irresistible) and I was certainly ardent: I didn't make a nuisance of myself, not until the end, anyway, and I never outstayed my welcome, not while there was still a welcome to be outstayed, but I was kind and sincere and thoughtful and devoted and I remembered things about her and I told her she was beautiful and bought her little presents that usually referred to a conversation we had had recently. None of this was an effort, of course, and none of it was done with any sense of calculation: I found it easy to remember things about her, because I didn't think about anything else, and I really did think she was beautiful, and I would not have been able to prevent myself from buying her little presents, and I did not have to feign devotion. There was no effort involved. So when one of Charlie's friends, a girl called Kate, said wistfully one lunchtime that she wished she could find somebody like me, I was surprised and thrilled. Thrilled because Charlie was listening, and it didn't do me any harm, but surprised because all I had done was act out of self-interest. And yet this was enough, it seemed, to turn me into someone desirable. Weird.
And, anyway, by moving to London I had made it easier to be liked by girls. At home, most people had known me, or my mum and dad – or had known somebody who knew me, or my mum and dad – when I was little, and consequently I'd always had the uncomfortable feeling that my boyhood was about to be exposed to the world. How could you take a girl out for an underage drink in a pub when you knew you had a scout uniform still hanging in your closet? Why would a girl want to kiss you if she knew (or knew somebody who knew) that just a few years before, you had insisted on sewing souvenir patches from the Norfolk Broads and Exmoor on your anorak? There were pictures all over my parents' house of me with big ears and disastrous clothes, sitting on tractors, clapping with glee as miniature trains drew into miniature stations; and though later on, distressingly, girlfriends found these pictures cute, it all seemed too close for comfort then.
It had only taken me six years to change from a ten-year-old to a sixteen-year-old; surely six years wasn't long enough for a transformation of that magnitude? When I was sixteen, that anorak with the patches on was just a couple of sizes too small.
Charlie hadn't known me as a ten-year-old, however, and she didn't know anybody who knew me, either. She knew me only as a young adult. I was already old enough to vote when I met her; I was old enough to

Annotations

- **9 strained** nervous, uneasy
- **14 ardour** passion, enthusiasm
- **15 make a nuisance of yourself** become a source of annoyance
- **16 outstay your welcome** stay longer than people want you to
- **17 sincere** honest and profound
- **18 devoted** loyal and committed
- **21 calculation** careful planning of your behaviour in order to achieve your aims
- **24 feign sth.** pretend to feel sth.
- **25 wistful** with regretful longing
- **33 expose sth.** show or reveal sth.
- **37 sew sth.** [səʊ] attach sth. with needle and thread
- **37 Norfolk Broads, Exmoor** national parks in England
- **41 glee** joy, delight
- **42 distressing** worrying
- **48 magnitude** degree, extent

Annotations

56 **hall of residence** university building with rooms for students
61 **fraud** pretender
63 **find sb. out** find out that sb. has a guilty secret or that they have been dishonest / not told the truth
64 **brandish sth.** wave sth.
65 **pack sb. in** (here) end the relationship
67 **St Albans** city north of London
69 **sophisticated** (here) mature

spend the night with her, the whole night, in her hall of residence, and have opinions, and buy her a drink in a pub, secure in the knowledge that my driving licence with its scrambled proof of age was in my pocket ... and I was old enough to have a history. At home I didn't have a history, just stuff that everybody already knew, and that therefore wasn't worth repeating.

But I still felt a fraud. I was like all those people who suddenly shaved their heads and said they'd always been punks, they'd been punks before punk was even thought of: I felt as though I was going to be found out at any moment, that somebody was going to burst into the college bar brandishing one of the anorak photos and yelling, 'Rob used to be a boy! A little lad!', and Charlie would see it and pack me in. It never occurred to me that she probably had a whole pile of pony books and some ridiculous party dresses hidden away at her parents' place in St Albans. As far as I was concerned, she had been born with enormous earrings, drainpipe jeans and an incredibly sophisticated enthusiasm for the works of some guy who used to splodge orange paint around.

We went out for two years, and for every single minute I felt as though I was standing on a dangerously narrow ledge. I couldn't ever get comfortable, if you know what I mean; there was no room to stretch out and relax. I was depressed by the lack of flamboyance in my wardrobe. I was fretful about my abilities as a lover. I couldn't understand what she saw in the orange paint guy, however many times she explained. I worried that I was never ever going to be able to say anything interesting or amusing to her about anything at all. I was intimidated by the other men on her design course, and became convinced that she was going to go off with one of them. She went off with one of them.

I lost the plot for a while then. And I lost the subplot, the script, the soundtrack, the intermission, my popcorn, the credits and the exit sign. I hung around Charlie's hall of residence until some friends of hers caught me and threatened to give me a good kicking. I decided to kill Marco (Marco!), the guy she went off with, and spent long hours in the middle of the night working out how to do it, although whenever I bumped into him I just muttered a greeting and sloped off. I did a spot of shoplifting, the precise motivation for which escapes me now. I took an overdose of Valium, and stuck a finger down my throat within a minute. I wrote endless letters to her, some of which I posted, and scripted endless conversations, none of which we had. And when I came round, after a couple of months of darkness, I found to my surprise that I had jacked in my course and was working in Record and Tape Exchange in Camden.

From: High Fidelity, *1995*

71 **splodge sth. around** smear sth. around
74 **ledge** edge of a cliff or windowsill
78 **flamboyance** spectacular extravagance
79 **fretful** uneasy, nervous
85 **intimidated** frightened
91 **intermission** break
95 **slope off** *(BE infml)* go away without attracting attention
95 **spot** *(n)* (here) a few cases
99 **come round** come to your senses again
100 **jack in sth.** *(BE infml)* give sth. up

Comprehension

► More info

1 Point out how the relationship with Charlie defines the *narrator's identity. Consider the narrator's preoccupation with being a 'fraud' (l. 61).

2 Summarize the narrator's social and emotional development over the episode.

Analysis

3 Examine how the author achieves comic or tragicomic effects. Consider his use of *irony, *register and *repetition.

► SF 18: Reading and understanding narrative texts, Student's book p. 286

Language awareness

4 Hornby's text features characteristic aspects of spoken language. Examples are the frequent use of phrasal verbs, interjections, colloquial expressions and repetitive patterns that often rely on stress.

Phrasal verb	Interjection	Colloquialism	Repetition
'turn ... into' (l. 28)	'Weird' (l. 29)	'tech' (l. 1)	'girl ... meet – meet girls' (ll. 2–3)
...	...	...	...

a Copy the table and fill in further examples from the text.
b Find less colloquial synonyms or rewrite at least two examples from each category in a more formal register.

Beyond the text

5 You choose Work on either **a** or **b**.

a Speaking After the break-up, the narrator lives through 'months of darkness' (l. 99), before finally dropping out of university. In groups, discuss what could be done to prevent such effects on one's life after a break-up.

b Writing Write one of the 'endless letters' (l. 97) the narrator writes in the aftermath of the break-up, either trying to make Charlie feel guilty for your misery or trying to win her back.

► Getting started (task a)
► SF 44: Having a discussion, Student's book p. 326
► SF 36: Creative writing, Student's book p. 311

Language help

It would be essential to ... • It might help to ... • It would do sb. good to ... • Another thing is ... • Well, I'd say ... • Personally, I think ... • If you ask me ...

Beauty ideals and social media

- Do you share pictures or videos on social media? What do you like about doing this, and what don't you like?
- What topics are trending on social media?

Comprehension

► SF 38: Listening/Viewing for gist and detail, Student's book p. 314

Annotations
vain extremely proud of your outer appearance, self-obsessed
roast sb. *(infml)* criticize sb.
catfish sb. *(infml)* trick sb. into a relationship by pretending to be someone else (esp. online)

1 Listening Watch the conversation of six teenagers about posting on social media. Take notes on the following aspects:

- importance of likes
- intentions when posting
- reactions to selfies
- opinions on vanity

Language awareness

2 a Viewing Watch the video again and take notes on nonverbal aspects of communication. Copy the table below and fill in your observations.

Aspect	Observations
Loudness	
*Pitch of voice	
Pauses and speed	
Gestures	
Facial expressions	
Eye contact	

b Examine how these nonverbal elements of communication add to meaning. Give examples.

Beyond the text

► Check

► SF 30: Writing an (online) article, Student's book p. 304

3 Work on either task **a** or **b**.

a For the English website of your school magazine, you have to prepare an article on beauty standards on social media and their potential risks. Collect and with a partner discuss the main points you want to make. Agree on pictures to illustrate your ideas.

b Challenge Writing Write an article for the English website of your school magazine dealing with beauty standards on social media and their potential risks.

4 Think back to the guiding question and consider if your views have changed, and how.

Art in Context: 'The fountain of youth' Lucas Cranach the Elder

▶ More info

- Talk with a partner: What makes being young attractive and what are the potential benefits of being old?

Then have a look at Lucas Cranach the Elder's painting 'The fountain of youth'.

Lucas Cranach the Elder: 'The fountain of youth', 1546

Comprehension

1 Describe the painting in detail.

▶ SF 22: Analysing visuals, Student's book p. 292

Analysis

2 Analyse how the painter manages to capture change in a static picture.

3 Explain the connection between youth, beauty and love implied in the painting. Also consider aspects of gender.

Beyond the text

4 Comment on the interdependence of youth, ideals of beauty and attempts at rejuvenation in this picture and relate it to the situation in modern western societies.

5 Based on your ideas from the pre-reading exercise, describe what a 'fountain of adulthood' might look like.

Info

Lucas Cranach the Elder (1472–1553) was a German painter and printmaker. He is best known for his portraits of German princes and the leaders of the Protestant Reformation (among them his friend Martin Luther) but also for mythological nudes.

Eternal youth?

▸ Getting started

- Speaking Work in groups of four and do a placemat activity. Each of you write down three characteristics young people shouldn't lose as they grow up. Then agree as a group on the three most important characteristics.

Partner B: Go to p. 26 and work on the tasks there.
Partner A: Read the text below and work on tasks 1 and 2.

Info

William Shakespeare (1564–1616) was an English poet, actor and playwright. He is famous for having written around 39 dramas and 154 sonnets. His sonnets follow a specific structure: in the first 12 lines (three quatrains) an idea is developed or a theory is discussed; the final couplet comes to a conclusion or a surprising turn. The speaker in his sonnets is an old poet.

Sonnet XVII William Shakespeare

Who will believe my verse in time to come
If it were filled with your most high deserts?
Though yet, heaven knows, it is but as a tomb
Which hides your life, and shows not half your parts.
If I could write the beauty of your eyes,
And in fresh numbers number all your graces,
The age to come would say, 'This poet lies;
Such heavenly touches ne'er touched earthly faces.'
So should my papers (yellowed with their age)
Be scorned, like old men of less truth than tongue,
And your true rights be termed a poet's rage
And stretchèd metre of an àntique song:
    But were some child of yours alive that time,
    You should live twice, in it and in my rhyme.

From: Sonnets, *1609*

Annotations
- 2 **deserts** *(pl)* (here) qualities
- 3 **tomb** sth. that is built over a place where a body has been laid
- 6 **graces** (here) elegant assets
- 8 **touch** *(n)* (here) feature
- 10 **scorn sth.** reject sth.
- 10 **tongue** (here) gossip
- 11 **termed** defined as, considered
- 11 **rage** (here) wild fantasy
- 12 **stretched** (here) exaggerated

Comprehension

1 Describe
- the concept of youth
- the dangers it faces
- ways to protect it from the dangers

presented in the *sonnet. Be prepared to present the results to your partner.

▸ SF 19: Reading and understanding poetry, Student's book p. 287

Analysis

2 a Examine the means Shakespeare uses to get his ideas across. Consider the sonnet's form and language.
b Choose three major aspects and be prepared to present them to your partner. Bear in mind that they do not know the poem.

▸ Getting started

3 a Exchange your findings on tasks 1 and 2 with your partner and listen to their findings.
b Together, discuss how the *stylistic devices in Shakespeare's poem and Dylan's song ensure they remain relevant today.

Beyond the text

4 With your partner, discuss whether you agree with the *speakers' views on youth presented in the sonnet and the song. You may also refer to your ideas from the pre-reading task and the painting by Lucas Cranach the Elder (cf. p. 19).

5 Writing Write a stanza or short poem in response to the song or the sonnet.

▸ SF 36: Creative writing, Student's book p. 311

Text 8

Lifelong lessons? Emma Jacobs

- Have you ever thought of doing a gap year after school? If so, what kind of gap year could you imagine? If not, why not?

Now read Emma Jacobs's account of her experiences as a gap-year student on a kibbutz in the Israeli desert.

For my generation, rising global temperatures are the norm and a clear threat to our future. [...] So it is important that we explore alternative, sustainable ways to live. That's why I'm spending my gap year learning how to farm in the desert and recycle poo.

Yeah, I know, gap yahs have been roundly mocked as the cliched preserve of those privileged youths who just want to 'discover themselves'. But studies have shown they can be good for personal development and teach skills that are beneficial at university and beyond.

So, along with 12 other teenagers, I'm spending a month on Kibbutz Lotan in the middle of the desert in southern Israel. We are a living social experiment: a self-sustaining, ecological 'village'. My home is a dome made of mud, clay, straw and a waterproofing layer of turpentine and recycled cooking oil, which I share with three others. It's a modern hut with a fan, plugs and even air-con. The village has compost toilets, solar showers, a sustainable kitchen with biogas and a bike-cum-washing machine that provides a work-out.

It's a massive change from the lives that most of us lead back in London. We've replaced Starbucks and shellac nails with shovels; it's taken some time to get over the culture shock.

Our days start with an 8 am wake-up: horribly early for me, but late for the real kibbutz workers who rise as early as 1 am to milk the cows. We start the chores before breakfast: cleaning the kitchen, loos and showers, and 'feeding' the biogas with yesterday's food scraps. After breakfast in the communal dining hall, we have permaculture and ecology lessons about the ethics of genetically modified crops, maintaining compost heaps, caring for the animals and keeping morale up throughout the long, hot days. We shovel goat and cow manure and build mud walls for the kibbutz kindergarten.

Working with animal dung is weirdly liberating for us townies. 'Being on kibbutz has made us feel less materialistic,' says participant Max Klass. He's never worked with animals before but says getting up close to the cows and goats is bringing out his 'rough and ready side'.

Annotations

4 **poo** *(infml)* solid end product of digestion
5 **gap yah** *(humorous)* gap year, i.e. period of time between finishing school and starting university
5 **mock sth.** make fun of sth.
5 **cliched** stereotypical
5 **preserve** *(n)* domain
10 **self-sustaining** maintaining itself independently
11 **dome** hut with a round roof
11 **clay** dried earth, often used to make bricks
12 **turpentine** oil distilled from certain trees
17 **shellac** (here) kind of nail polish
17 **shovel** tool used to move earth
22 **scrap** bit of food left over
23 **permaculture** sustainable agriculture
23 **crop** *(n)* fruit, grain or vegetable won by harvest
24 **morale** good spirit, confidence
25 **manure** waste matter from animals used to fertilize the soil to make plants grow

Annotations
31 feat great accomplishment
37 utopia imaginary perfect world
40 dairy building where milk products are processed

A simpler, more sustainable, ecologically ethical lifestyle is an achievable feat if you start on a small scale, adds participant Dan Apter. 'People don't know that shovelling shit is such fun.'

I've found there's more to the kibbutz experience than just an ecological education. We're learning to live a truly communal life. It can be tough, but living in an 'intentional community' feels like valuable training for university and a life of work. Yet even in this utopia, the books have to balance. Like many kibbutzim nowadays, this one has been privatised to ensure its economic survival. But it is still a place where members debate issues such as whether it's ethical to maintain a refet (dairy), the extent of communal responsibility, and how to fairly distribute resources.

This time next year, I'll be at Leeds University. I may not need to pick dates, farm or manage a compost loo there, but I'll take the broader lessons that I'm learning on the kibbutz with me. I know it will affect the decisions I make about all sorts of things, from which products to buy to how to use transport. And it's given me all kinds of ideas for the future.

From: 'Gap year stories: getting a taste of communal living', theguardian.com, *2 January 2017*

Comprehension

1 Make notes on the following aspects mentioned in the text:
1. Two contrasting views on gap years: ...
2. The volunteers' living conditions: ...
3. The volunteers' daily tasks: ...
4. The volunteers' attitude to their tasks:
5. Topics dealt with in their ecological education: ...
6. The effect that living on a kibbutz has had on Emma: ...

Analysis

2 Contrast positive and negative aspects of life at Kibbutz Lotan and examine how their representation supports the author's message.

Language awareness

▸ More language

3 The writer makes frequent use of *informal words or expressions. For example, instead of the standard 'gap year', she uses 'gap yah' (l. 5), which imitates a posh accent and is mildly mocking.

a Explain the following words and expressions, inferring their meaning from their parts or from their context:
1. 'air-con' (l. 13)
2. 'bike-cum-washing machine' (l. 14)
3. '[one's] rough and ready side' (l. 30)
4. 'the books have to balance' (l. 37)

b Find other examples of informal words or expressions and say whether you find them suitable for a quality newspaper like the *Guardian*. Change two of them into a more *formal style and explain how this changes their meaning.

Beyond the text

4 You choose Work on either task **a** or **b**.

a Speaking You are a representative of an organization that arranges gap years for students. Prepare and give a talk for a study fair aimed at international students. Make sure to present the benefits of gap years. Refer to Emma Jacobs's account, but add ideas of your own.

b Writing Write an online *article on life after school for your school's website. Discuss the benefits and drawbacks of gap years and present other ideas for the future focusing on your local community.

▸ Getting started

▸ SF 42: Preparing and giving a speech, Student's book p. 324

▸ SF 30: Writing an (online) article, Student's book p. 304

Text 9

Routes into work

Tess Reidy

▸ More info

- Have you already decided on what to do after school? Note down one course at university, one apprenticeship trade and one internship programme that might suit you if you were to launch a career now. Give reasons.
- Compare lists with other students and discuss the reasons for your choices.

Now read the text about the pros and cons of internships, apprenticeships and university courses.

It can feel like there's a lot to think about for job seekers during summer: top employers are on the lookout for interns, grad schemes are available in everything from banking to retail, and with more than 1,500 job roles to choose from, there is a wide range of apprenticeships to consider.
To get you focused, here's a myth-busting guide on what to consider before you commit to a career.

Internships don't pay

Unpaid internships are illegal, and most people doing any kind of work experience for longer than two weeks are entitled to the national minimum wage. In fact, law firms, banks and consultancy firms can pay as much as £500 per week for vacation schemes.

Although they typically last for one to three months, there's a growing number advertised for up to a year, and they have become a way to impress employers and figure out what suits you.

Unfortunately, many companies still offer them unpaid or run them under the guise of volunteer work. 'In the arts, there is this genuine belief that you are lucky to have one because 100 other people have applied,' says Millie Jones*, 21, who did a four-month unpaid internship for a film festival. 'You can end up doing 16 hour days. I felt I couldn't say no or put my foot down because I didn't want to lose the contract.'

Annotations

2 **grad scheme** *(infml)* = graduate scheme, special employment contract for sb. who has just completed a university course

3 **retail** *(n)* sale of goods, e.g. in shops

5 **myth-busting** correcting false beliefs

9 **be entitled to sth.** have a legal right to sth.

9 **wage** regular payment from employer

10 **consultancy firm** business that offers expert advice

10 **vacation scheme** period of work experience offered to students

15 **under the guise of sth.** taking on the form or appearance of sth.

16 **volunteer** *(n)* sb. who agrees to work without compensation

19 **put your foot down** adopt a strong position

Annotations
- **23 do maintenance** perform a caretaker's tasks
- **29 solicitor** legal professional dealing with legal documents e.g. for selling buildings
- **30 accountant** professional in the financial sector
- **33 degree-level** *(adj)* on the same level as an academic degree
- **33 incur debt** owe sb. money
- **37 craft** *(n)* trade that requires skillful working with hands
- **42 offset** beginning
- **51 vacancy** job offer
- **52 consecutive** following each other directly, without interruption

Jones, who was not paid expenses, funded herself with a childcare job at the weekends and evenings. She thinks employers take advantage of people like her. 'One intern ended up doing maintenance round the office, like changing light bulbs,' she says.

Apprenticeships are low-level

People often think apprenticeships are just for specific trades, such as construction, or that they are in some way not academic. This isn't true. They cover a range of sectors and levels. Over the past decade, they have become an alternative to academic education and there are now apprenticeship routes into becoming a solicitor, an accountant, an engineer, or business manager.

According to Stephen Isherwood from the Institute of Student Employers, many high-profile companies now recruit apprentices. 'Apprenticeships offer the opportunity to gain a degree-level qualification whilst working and not incurring student debt,' he says.

You can also end up being the boss. 'A large number of business leaders in the sector are former apprentices themselves', says David Fagan from Make UK, who points out that the average pay for a craft apprentice is £11,000, rising to £20,000 in the fourth year.

Apprentices miss out on the uni experience

True, as an apprentice you'll enter the world of work earlier than your uni mates. You'll also be trained very specifically within a sector, so you need to be dedicated to that from the offset. But this doesn't mean you won't be part of a shared experience. Most organisations take on more than one apprentice, so you will usually have a network of similar aged colleagues.

Corey Bueno-Ballantyne, a mechanical engineering apprentice from Telford, says a big part of going to uni is making friends and you get that from apprenticeships. 'We're together every day, we go out for drinks,' he says. 'We spent our first and second years living together in a hotel.'

Grad schemes are for recent grads

Getting hired is competitive. According to the Institute of Student Employers there are 41 applications for every graduate vacancy. A common misconception is if you don't get one straight away, you've missed out. Plenty of people apply for consecutive years, do a post-university gap year, or even work in a different sector before starting a grad scheme.

'It's likely you'll start your grad scheme with lots of young people who have just graduated, but you don't have to be fresh out of uni to do one,' says Becky Kells, editor of AllAboutSchoolLeavers.

**Name changed for confidentiality*

From: 'Internship, grad scheme or apprenticeship – which route into work is best?', theguardian.com, *9 July 2019*

Comprehension

1 Note down key words on what the text tells us about
1 internships (4 aspects)
2 apprenticeships (4 aspects)
3 grad schemes (2 aspects)

Analysis

2 Analyse the means the writer employs to catch the reader's attention.

Language awareness

3 In order to introduce direct quotes in the text, the writer almost exclusively uses forms of *say* (cf. ll. 17, 24, 34, 36, 45, 47, 56). Rewrite these sentences using more meaningful verbs from the box below.

point out that … • claim that … • make clear that … • doubt that … • add that … • remember that … • maintain that … • clarify that … • believe that … • concede that

Beyond the text

4 Speaking | Intercultural communication For an international school partnership, you are requested to produce a short informative video clip comparing routes into work in Germany and in an English-speaking country of your choice.
a Research similarities and differences in both countries, then with a partner agree on the information you want to include.
b Choose pictures and write the lines of text that convey your ideas.
c Either make the film clip or draw the storyboard and present it in class.

► Check
► SF 12: Communicating across cultures, Student's book p. 277

Chapter task

Prepare a short message to your future self, spoken or written, reminding yourself of aspects of young life that should never be forgotten.

► Getting started

Text 3

▸ p. 14

Is 'OK, Boomer' ok, Boomer?

1 Support

List things Rezo criticizes about the Boomer generation and their way of communicating.

Text 7

▸ p. 20

Eternal youth?

Partner B

Info

Bob Dylan (born 1941) is a famous US-American singer and songwriter who composed music of various genres including Folk, Blues, Rock, Country, Pop and Gospel. The musician became an icon of the civil rights and peace movements in the 1960s due to his songs about racism, social inequality and war. The song 'Blowin' in the Wind' even became a hymn of the protest movement. In 2016 he was the first musician to be awarded the Nobel prize for literature.

Annotations
6 **rung** crosspiece of a ladder
10 **righteous** virtuous, ethical
20 **swift** quick, fast

Forever young Bob Dylan

May God bless and keep you always
May your wishes all come true
May you always do for others
And let others do for you
May you build a ladder to the stars
And climb on every rung
May you stay forever young
Forever young, forever young
May you stay forever young

May you grow up to be righteous
May you grow up to be true
May you always know the truth
And see the lights surrounding you
May you always be courageous
Stand upright and be strong
May you stay forever young

Forever young, forever young
May you stay forever young
May your hands always be busy
May your feet always be swift
May you have a strong foundation
When the winds of changes shift
May your heart always be joyful
May your song always be sung
Forever young, forever young
May you stay forever young

From: Planet Waves, *1974*

Comprehension

1 Describe the concept of youth presented in the song. Be prepared to present the results to your partner.

2 **a** Examine the means Dylan uses to get his ideas across. Consider the song's form and language.

b Choose three major aspects and be prepared to present them to partner A. Bear in mind that they do not know the poem.

Now go back to task 3 on p. 20.

Cover
stock.adobe.com/Katarzyna Leszczynsk

Photos
pp. 4/5 woman with headphones: Shutterstock.com/insta_photos, volunteers: Shutterstock.com/Dmytro Zinkevych; **p. 5** classroom: Shutterstock.com/Monkey Business Images, protest: Shutterstock.com/Paapaya, basketball game: stock.adobe.com/Marcos, IT job: mauritius images/Rupert Oberhäuser; **p. 6 top**: mauritius images/alamy stock photo/Kuttig – Archival, bottom: mauritius images/Westend61; **p. 7**: stock.adobe.com/Jan H. Andersen; **p. 8** image a: Shutterstock.com/Duet PandG, image b: mauritius images/age footstock, image c: mauritius images/alamy stock photo/Sally and Richard Greenhill, image d: mauritius images/TopFoto, image e: mauritius images/alamy stock photo/BWAC Images, image f: mauritius images/Collection Christophel, image g: ClipDealer GmbH/Andrey Armyagov, image h: Shutterstock.com/WUT.ANUNAI, image i: mauritius images/TopFoto, image j: mauritius images/alamy stock photo/Hager fotografie, image k: mauritius images/alamy stock photo/Sally and Richard Greenhill, image l: stock.adobe.com/Inti St. Clair; **p. 10**: Shutterstock.com/Monkey Business Images; **p. 11**: mauritius images/Image Source; **p. 12**: Shutterstock.com/GaudiLab; **p. 15**: Shutterstock.com/thinkhubstudio; **p. 16**: mauritius images/és collection; **p. 17**: Shutterstock.com/Wachiraphorn Thongya; **p. 19**: Bridgeman Images/Cranach, Lucas the Elder, Fountain of Youth (1546); **p. 20**: Shutterstock.com/ArtMari; **p. 22**: mauritius images/alamy stock photo/Independent Picture Service; **p. 25** top: Shutterstock.com/Monkey Business Images, centre: Shutterstock.com/ESB Professional, bottom: Shutterstock.com/Rawpixel.com

Texts
pp. 10–11: Iqbal, Nosheen. "Generation Z - Are the kids alright?", *theguardian.com*, 21 July 2018, https://www.theguardian.com/society/2018/jul/21/generation-z-has-different-attitudes-says-a-new-report (accessed 30.09.2021), Copyright Guardian News & Media Ltd 2021; **pp. 13–14**: "OK, Boomer" ist okay, Boomer! *ZEIT ONLINE*, Eine Kolumne von Rezo, 20.11.2019, https://www.zeit.de/kultur/2019-11/generationenkonflikt-ok-boomer-millenials-babyboomer-rezo/komplettansicht (Zugriff 23.07.2021); **pp. 14–16**: Hornby, Nick. *High Fidelity*. London, Penguin Books, 2000, pp. 15-17; **pp. 21–22**: Jacobs, Emma and Hickford, Sam. "Gap year stories: getting a taste of communal living", *theguardian.com*, 2 Jan 2017, https://www.theguardian.com/education/2017/jan/02/gap-year-stories-getting-a-taste-of-communal-living (accessed 23.07.2021), Copyright Guardian News & Media Ltd 2021; **pp. 23–24**: Reidy, Tess. "Internship, grad scheme or apprenticeship - which route into work is best?", *theguardian.com*, 9 July 2019, https://www.theguardian.com/careers/2019/jul/09/internship-grad-scheme-or-apprenticeship-which-route-into-work-is-best (accessed 20.09.2021), Copyright Guardian News & Media Ltd 2021.

Song
p. 26 *Forever Young*. Ram-s-Horn-Music/Dwarf Music Sony/ATV Publishing (Germany GmbH), Dylan, Bob